Friedrich Pancratius

Alwilda

or, her first holy communion and A Christmas carol

Friedrich Pancratius

Alwilda

or, her first holy communion and A Christmas carol

ISBN/EAN: 9783741193774

Manufactured in Europe, USA, Canada, Australia, Japa

Cover: Foto ©Lupo / pixelio.de

Manufactured and distributed by brebook publishing software (www.brebook.com)

Friedrich Pancratius

Alwilda

Ernest's Visit.

AH! welcome, Friend! how sweet, that you have come
To while away the hours this winter-night;
What joy to think how we as children roamed
Absorbing nature's glee in passing time.
Oft, when fatigued, I in this chair would sit,
O'erpondering our youthful pleasant games,
My heart desired to roam with you once more.
But all is changed! you grew so stout and strong,
And your bright eyes, do make my soul rejoice.

Be seated now beside the warming fire,
Else winter's icy frost our bones will shake;
Just listen how the storm-wind howling blows
And sips the heat from out this burning log.
Does he not summon to the welcome hearth
Each loving soul, a legend them to tell?
The window-panes he covers with a veil
Of flowers, rich in beautiful design,
Which cheerily reflect the rising flames;
The trees are heard a-weeping and they crack
As if they'd care no more to live their day.
The storm-wind's raging fury being spent,

The cold, cold air then fills all crevices,
With no regard for poor or suffering ones.
Let's stir the log; the cold my blood does chill
And draws the blanket tighter 'round my back.

These flames, which in their crackling noise ascend,
And then sink back into a slumb'ring dream,
From which they start with even greater strength,
With their surroundings lend their aid
To ev'ry object, which we may behold,
And like the scenery the drama helps.
So they assistance give this lovely tale.
Their shadows, ah! from darkest into light,
Are necessary adjuncts, as you know.
Thus, glimm'ring log brings visions of the past
Which, sad'ning in effect, but full of peace,
Are leaving in their fleeing, a desire
For the return of dear ones, gone before,
Who in their love endeared the hearth to us.

Come closer now, that we each other's life
Can well peruse and thus live o'er again,
With all the ups and downs, as rise these flames
And sinking coil themselves in welcome rest.
You Ernest! came in quest of precious love
Of whom I have this legend now to tell.
Be patient! hear me well unto the end,
Whilst good Alwilda helps me to relate
The sad but happy tidings of her life.

The Emerald.

THERE is a lovely hill, which over all
　　The country 'round a panoramic view
Commands, with ever new and changing scene,
So elevating to the inner soul
That we in holy wonderment exclaim,
Most surely God his beauty here impressed.
Refreshed by spring-times green, the stately trees
With lofty crowns their shadows throw
O'er the inviting soft and velvet lawn.
The silv'ry rivulet reflects so mild
The setting sun's last wish for a sweet rest,
And lures from park, enriched with flowered plants,
The happy birdlings song, good night, good night!
All join to heighten nature's blessèd joy
Inviting old and young to this hill-top,
Where they may rest on shapely rustic seat
And drink with pleasure ev'nings gentle breeze.
Here stands the mansion Emerald we call,
Of granite built, scarce showing through the green,
With fancy windows, gables and high peaks.
It's spacious rooms, well-lighted, welcome us

As we are gently ushered through them all,
The large reflecting mirror's grand display
Of Carpets, Furniture and Tapestry,
Depicts a scene, that calls for praise.

Here, where the angels nursing play, was born
Alwilda, of all fairies the most fair.

Alwilda's Childhood.

WHEN pleasant spring-days their appearance make,
Then from their winter's sleep awakening
The trees their cheery blossoms hold to view
And luscious plants exert themselves in growth
To play their proudest colors to the sun.
And these succeeding with deserved success
Unite Rose, Lily and Forget-me-not
With myriads of others of their kin
In happy blending to a sweet bouquet.
Thus they perfume the gentle kissing breeze
To bring the feathered dwellers of the woods,
The happy birds, with plumage rich and fair
And song so sweet, that we would fain desire
To have them while with us forever here.

But no! the welcome warm and pleasant sun,
To whom the grateful flowers raised their heads,
With a sarcastic smile sends down his rays
Of burning heat to sip their sap of life.
Thus injured, hurt, the stricken plants bend low,
Regretting life and wither in decay.

The little bird, which with bewitching song,
Had lured us near and nearer to his perch,
With caution turns, as we would speak to him,
And mercilessly flies away from us.

Alwilda grew in body and in mind
Impressing favorably ev'ry one;
She practised all the noble virtues taught
By her good mother's word and holy life.
Hence she was chosen by the young to be
Their central figure, which they would respect,
Obey and love, whereas the parents all
In conversation loved to speak of her.

The fleety spring into ripe summer grows,
And so the child its careless playground leaves
To go to school. The blood more quiet now,
The little brain is fed with mental food
For earthly welfare and eternal bliss.
Alwilda's talent, industry and love,
Attracted all the children close to her.
And though she never sought the pleasing praise,
When school was over, she would hurry home
And kneeling, with her hands upon the lap
Of her good mother, she would then relate
With open eye and placid countenance
All whatsoever had that day occurred.
She listened then attentively to all
Her mother Peregrina had to say

Of vanity and pride, of beauty, wealth,
And even of the great and learned minds;
Yes, how but one thing happiness creates:
To love the God, who placed us in this world
And who prepares a crown for future time.
Alwilda promised, and her promise kept,
That from the path of virtue and of truth
She'd never stray; and with a gentle kiss
Arose to help her mother in her work.

Fernando and Peregrina.

THE shining sun the worthy task fulfills,
   Which holy Providence has set for him;
And not a tree could stand majestic there,
Nor could a plant existence e'er enjoy,
Nor seed of any kind, so hopeful sown,
Could show a healthy growth to searching eye,
Were it not for that warm encouragement.

'Tis true, old sol so often sullen looks,
And in his anger vexes ev'ry one;
When going into passion's greatest heat
He trickles from his brow the drops of sweat
And forces all their shelter seek in shade.

In his great fury he would ruin all,
Forgetting his own fate, if left alone;
But God in holy wisdom, knowing this,
Gave him as consort sweet and ever-good
The pacifying silver-facéd moon,
Who both with winning smile and moving tears
Implores for peace and harmony at home,
And calleth in her children, little stars.

To show them to her king in happy love,
And after this to send them to their rest.

Fernando's giant form was ev'rywhere,
Where helping hand was being sought,
And with impatience he would push
Through ev'ry obstacle, that showed itself.
Such energy suggests the true success,
But also likens nature's wildest stream,
Which may some day break through its banks
And overflow the country far and wide,
Destroying all the fruit of labors toil.

Now prudent Peregrina, unobserved,
Held anxious watch o'er him in such a mood
And with foreboding fear she knelt to pray,
That God would help to lead her husband right.

Fernando's work was done and to his home
He turned his steps to rest from his day's work.
Before he reached the mansion-stair, his wife
Came with the lightest treads of love to greet
And welcome his return. With gentle hand
She stroked his hair and with her mildest words
She opened his big heart to her own love.
Fernando's noble soul in gratitude
Preserved the mem'ry of her kindly deed.

When in the ev'ning breeze they slowly strolled
Out in the garden lane, the visitors
Would stand a blessing to implore,
Whilst in their heart they longed their peace to
        share.

The Tavern.

THE sweetest home is insufficient oft
   To satisfy the pleasure-seeking heart
And out into the woods and wild we roam
To chase with danger the uncertain game.
We care not for the rocks and rills, nor for
The fallen trees and underbrush, but leap
O'er these in hot pursuit; and all for joy!
Our legs may ache, our backs be sore, our dogs
May bleeding lie and gored: it's our delight!
The downy cot at home is changed for lawn,
Exacting meals for piece of hardened bread
And sparkling water fills the place of wine;
For canopy we have the clouded sky.

The hardships of the chase invigorate
And blind the yearning heart to threat'ning harm.
For surely blind it is to pay a price,
Which never hare was worth in hist'ry's time,
And which is truly frequently the case.
It is a whim! The hunter has his fun
But fun which hardest work for him contains;

And when perhaps he sees the hare escape:
How sweet to say, he almost caught the same!

These whims, enjoyments, call them what you may,
Are present in some form in everyone;
And though encouraging the human heart,
Whenever right and prudently employed,
They will however certain ruin bring
O'er those, who let them to a passion grow
Now passion, like a fire, creates a draft,
Wherewith it fans itself to greater heat,
And leaping seeks more fuel to attract.
The hunter has his joy with comrades gay
Who, when they cannot hunt, will oft convene,
And, passing 'round the flask, will tell their tales,
Or sitting down will kill the time with cards.
But play is dry, the tongue needs loosening,
And so the mug is passed around, around!
The game grows weary, losing all its warmth,
Wherefore a stake is set upon the same.
We've heard: from little acorns big trees grow,
So smallest coin takes on a golden hue!
At first the joy of winning driveth on
And next revenge for losing is the cause,
That with relentless zeal the play is pushed,
Repeating this as time its circle turns,
From day to night and from the night to morn.
No thought is had of one another's loss

Of hard-earned cash; the business goes down
Because the master is too busy sure;
And wife and child henceforth neglected are,
For better friends, he claims, are holding him.

Fernando's fate was moulded just this way,
And from the restful recreation sprang
The passion, which soon generated ill
And ruin brought upon the entire house.

Down in the valley, where the mud is deep
A house appears, quite darkened with the time,
Whose uncleansed windows purposely are screened,
Thus making dust and dirt more plainly seen.
But screened they are, like those who pull their hats
Deep down to hide their conscience-stricken eye;
Thus imitating that long-leggéd bird,
Of richest feather's fame, but not of wits'
Aside this house, if house it may be called,
A low unseemly pen is kept
Alive with constant grunting of a hog,
Which shoves in greedy search its poking snoot
Into the mud with greatest appetite;
Occasionally lying down to rest
Right in the centre of its meanly pool.
The water trough in front would make a horse
Show his disgust by wagging his wise head;
The place is so abhorrent, that we'd say,

No self-respecting man would tarry here.
But let us drown disgust and enter in:
We now behold a counter, of all polish bare
A table weather-worn, 'round which four chairs
Lie in disorder; and with nausea
We step the unwashed floor; the broken walls
Are lined with some few shelves, which serve
To bring to mind the mem'ries of the past.
These very walls, with plaster broken spots
And other markings, give much food for thought.
The mediæval crucifix has fled
And not a vestige good has here remained.
The hunters gathering enjoyed at home
Was soon embarrassed at the kind restraint,
Which Peregrina prudently employed
And hence recourse was had to that dark inn,
Where kind solicitude of his good wife
Was sentenced to oblivion, at first
Most sparse, then gradually more and more
Until the once so fondling love transformed
Into the selfish instinct of the brute.
His former gentleness was so transformed,
That Peregrina feared his presence much;
The open mien half-closed its once-fair eyes,
And the erect and noble frame caved in
Its mighty chest and stooped the shoulders deep;
The strongly sinewed legs refused to bear
The body's weight, and staggered to and fro,

Whilst for support he reaches for the air,
Which in revenge vibrates the laughing nerves
Of standersby and then fills with contempt
Or pity ev'ry sympathizing heart.
The waves of drink, a syphon drawing all,
Have drawn into the depth, whence no return,
Wealth and success, health, happiness and peace!

No mortal tongue is able to describe
The anguish of a woman's troubled heart
Beholding, how the storm-clouds rising gray,
Contract in blackest hue, dispelling light
And ever ready with a roar to burst
Into a flashing stroke their vengeful spite.
She, Peregrina knew, though rich they were,
That for a paltry sum a mortgage lay
Upon their stately home, a trifle once,
But now a burden, which they could not bear.
In earnest prayer bent she knelt for hours
And many were the tears she sadly wept,
But not so much for fear the home to lose;
She knew that happiness was not in wealth,
But in the hearts content and holy love;
Though humbled, she would sacrifice her all,
If only he returned to love again.
Still more, he had a soul, which she would save,
For heaven's everlasting happiness;
And so she wept and prayed and prayed and wept,

That he from evil ways would soon convert.
Her lovely winning face its color lost,
Her big blue eyes were dimmed and red with tears.
And thus the everpleasant smiling moon
Became a dreary wand'rer of the night.
Sore in her knees, she slowly paced the floor,
Ejaculating sorrows to the sky,
As if to force a pity for her plight.
It seemed in vain! From ruin ruin comes:
The time is past, nor can the debt be paid!

Yon clouds had burst with their accustomed crash
And spent their vengeance with a crushing force;
Fernando looked bedazed, but was too weak
To bear it bravely, and dejected went
To drown it's mem'ry in the curséd inn!

The Hut in the Woods.

SIX years have since that fatal day elapsed.
    Years, which with time increased the
        sore distress
Of Peregrina's good but bleeding heart.
The misery which she did undergo
In consequence of law's tight-clinching hand
Defies description, taking all desire
Of life away; she only lived in faith,
That soon the end of earthly time would come
To open heaven's gates beyond the grave.
She sighed most piteously, that God would grant,
That this most longed-for hour would soon arrive:
And yet she prayed and prayed for death to wait
Until Fernando would go better ways.

She swooned when carried from her pleasant home
And on this couch she lay apparent dead;
Alwilda o'er her lying wept so much,
That we believed her youthful heart would break.
When Peregrina's strength again returned,
She thanked so earnestly for all the care,

Which I was happy to bestow on her,
And rising, with Alwilda, would have gone,
From door to door, in search of hardened bread,
For which she'd offer work, as best she could.
Myself, as you are well aware, too poor
To keep her here and to provide for all,
I yet could not consider such a thought
Of seeing her go begging o'er the land.
She finally agreed with me to stay
Until a hut I'd built some distance out,
Where she could live in peace and with her work
Provide for her support, whilst I would try
To bring Fernando back to common sense.
It seemed to come our way. Fernando was
Now softened and remembering his wife
And child, he brooding stared into the world.
He startled, almost frightened when I spoke
But gladdened much at the proposal made;
Himself would help to built this humble hut
Resolving better life henceforth to lead.
No brighter cloud could after storm appear,
Nor could a consolation more console,
Than by this news our lady was rejoiced.
The followmorn with axe and saw and square
We went a distance out into the woods;
Though sad, there never was a sweeter work,
Than when with all our might we felled the trees,
Which cut to equal length we straightway laid

In form of square securing end to end.
And piling them on all sides in their turn
Till to the roof, which we with shingles laid;
The windows, rather low, were six in all,
Three in the front, and in the rear wall three;
Two rooms, one large, one small, the house contained.
The oaken bedstead, which stood at the wall,
The rounded table and three common chairs
Together with an ancient cooking stove
And a few dishes had been left to them.
All was prepared, so Peregrina left
With heartfelt thanks for what my duty was;
She felt so happy now, that I was forced
To turn away and hide my pressing tears,
Whilst praying God fore'er to be with them!

Not many days had passed before I saw
Fernando in a gloomy mood go home;
His wife somehow all day dejected felt
But knew it not to be presentiment.
Fernando took a seat upon a stone
And brooding brooded ever more, and this
Made Peregrina fear and worry much;
She begged and cried for him to change his mood.
But no! instead, he answered with a snarl.

A crucifix, the one my mother pressed
Upon her lips, when God did call her soul,

And which I prized above all other gifts
As her last proof of love. I loaned to her
Upon her pleading tears; may it console
Her future, as it helped her in the past.
Before this holy cross she kneeling prayed,
That God in mercy would debar all harm;
She prayed for him who nearest stood to her,
And offered her own child as sacrifice.
She felt composed and strengthened after this;
Whereas Fernando hardened in his sin
By daily visits to that robber's den,
Which brought such misery upon his head
And where the scanty earnings of his wife
Were rushing down the throat in draughts of drink
Thus new and harder trials o'er her came
And though they brought a flow of bitter tears
Still, Peregrina bore them patiently
And felt assured, that all would yet end well.

Alwilda, seeing mother's great distress,
Endeavored anxiously to give relief
By word and deed and ev'ry proof of love;
And when the child felt gloomy, she was seen
To gain new strength by crossing her good breast
And driving evil powers far away.
And then she smiled the sweetest angel's smile
For sweeter lips you never could have seen.

Alwilda's Dream.

THE days of trial fled, like those of joy,
   And sad and dreary, as they ever were,
They still were bright, because of inner strength
Imparted by the graceful hand of God.
Like precious gold, which must be purified
In fire's most fiercely burning blaze and heat,
Or else it's quality would ne'er appear;
So too, hard sufferings for men will mould
The perfect qualities for greatness true,
Nor can a man be great without the same.
Again, it's easy to be virtuous,
So long our nature's flattered doing good.
But what, amid most dire adversity,
When not a ray of hope can be observed
Except in trust and confidence in God ?
Therefore the saints their life in suff'ring spent
And martyrs by the million bear their palm,
All giving testimony to our Lord,
Who dragged his heavy cross to Calvary.
"In meekness hidden lieth perfect strength

And through the week the strong confounded are,"
As the apostle of the Gentiles says.
Our Saviour by his death upon the cross
O'ercame his enemies, world, satan, sin,
And with his poor apostles, only twelve,
He raised the entire sunken universe.
We find, not only in the moral world
This lesson taught, that crowns must well be earned,
And earned by test of hardest trials too.
The vegetable kingdom even gives
Abundant proof to us of this same fact;
The cutting and transplanting of the plant
And all the treatment which it must receive,
Insure the sturdy growth in symmetry;
But left alone and sure a dwarf appears
In wildness stretching armlike o'er the ground.
Now God knows best, and as we e'er behold,
That in probations He His saints does try
And through the prophet's word revealed.
That He chastises whomsoe'er He loves.
So we can understand why pious souls,
Though innocent, must suffer e'er so much;
And if the trial springs from nature's course,
Then God will grant new blessings to the soul
And cause a brighter crown prepared for her,
Provided, she will bear all patiently;
So was it from beginning of the world,
So will it be until the close of time.

When Peregrina reigned in peaceful wealth,
She numbered friends by many scores;
We daily see the same without surprise,
But, says the German proverb, well and true :
"Distress around, Friends, hundred to a pound;"
Or, as the poet, Goldsmith, puts it well:

> And what is Friendship, but a name,
> A charm that lulls to sleep,
> A shade that follows wealth or fame
> And leaves the wretch to weep.

Yea, all these countless friends their color changed
And turned, I dare say, to so many fiends,
"To kick," the saying goes, "the dog that's down;"
The one proclaimed, we see it plainly now,
Not all that glitters is of solid gold;
Another knew, from private source, the wealth
Fernando sadly lost had been ill-gained;
Again: it's Peregrina's boasting pride
And her own secret sins, that ruin wrought.
It was the gossip at the teas, the talk
At ev'ry corner in the town, and when
On Sundays from the house of God they'd come
You'd notice them their dirty tales exchange,
And winking, squinting, speaking extra loud
To make it hurt and cut the woman's heart, —
But she with dear Alwilda hurried home.

No sooner had they reached their lonely hut,
When Peregrina sank upon the couch,

No longer able to hold back her tears,
As if her fitful sighs would bring relief.
She gladly would have suffered all alone,
But that her darling child should feel it too
Was more than her maternal heart could bear.
Alwilda witnessing her great distress
Knelt down before her, pleaded, wept and begged
Her to forget it all and be consoled,
As she an angel-message would confide:
It was a dream, but one that God had sent.
The mother woke as startled by a touch,
And with a sorrowful, but smiling look
Embraced her child and lightly kissed
The forehead of her sweet dear little one;
She bade her then proceed.

    Alwilda said:
"When we had left the rich and pleasant home
And you were lying in a swoon, like dead,
I threw myself upon you in my grief
And prayed and prayed; I thought my heart would
                  break.
I fell asleep and music, oh! so sweet!
Then came unto my ears; at once there shone
A brightness, which became e'er brighter still.
I felt so happy, but too weak to lift
My head and look: A gentle hand then touched
And raised me up, and there! my Angel stood

Before me; — oh! how beautiful he was!
I see him yet! — I raised by hands and prayed
And begged him kindly let me go with him.
The angel pointed then to you and said:
Not yet! and with this all had disappeared.

Another dream I had; it was the night
When father, sitting on a stone, was sad;
You knelt to pray and rose so full of peace.
My heart was heavy and I prayed so hard,
That my good angel would give joy to you.
I fell asleep; again the music came
And so the brightness and the angel too.
I raised my hands and prayed for father dear,
That he would henceforth leave his wicked ways.
The angel spoke so sweet, and smiling said,
That on a certain day he would convert,
And with a blessing left me in my sleep."

Alwilda having finished sank in thought,
As if an angel's secret she betrayed,
But soon felt satisfied, as she beheld
Her mother well consoled, (o'erpondering
Each word she heard from good Alwilda's lips.)

The Village Priest.

PROSPERITY has always had distastes,
Whilst comforts season the adversities
And consolations crown the greatest griefs.
Oft guests most pleasantly invited are
'Though really their absence is desired;
And then again, it great relief bestows
To tell to friends the sorrows of one's heart,
Thus making sympathy help bear the same.
Saint Paul, by word and deed this lesson taught,
That he grew warm when others vexèd were.
And since his day the zealous priests of God
Have had their sympathy for ev'ryone.
Instinctively the faithful find their friend —
The one they lovingly their Father name,
Because a father's heart is given him
By God, who for his people thus provides,
That bended reed may not be broken off.
'Tis true the father sometimes stern must be,
But when repentance shows, he kind forgives
And helps to raise the deeply humbled soul.

When Peregrina heard the darling's dream
She pondered much, but all seemed mystery.
And so she went fo Father Coelestine,
For by this name the village priest was known,
And opened up her anguished heart to him;
It was, indeed, the wisest thing to do!
The priest, so venerable in his ways,
With all the charity, that grace bestows,
And humble meekness, and affection true
Was well deserving of her confidence.
His life-long study of the human soul,
Assisted by a rich experience
Of many years with ev'ry class of men;
Again, the very office he doth fill,
Insuring him God's grace to counsel right
The haunted, troubled or doubt-stricken soul,
Must naturally bring the sore-distressed,
Appealing, to his welcome cottage door.
And this the more, as the infusèd faith
Is followed by the reverential awe
With noble trust in God's self-chosen priest.
There never was a people in the world,
Who do not testify to this known fact,
And all the ages of the universe
Show plainly the respect and trust in him.
They say in peril we will learn to pray,
And likewise the unwilling will yet go
To him who after all is their best friend.

When Peregrina rang the tiny bell
She greeted with the blessèd Christian's call
Of 'Praised be Jesus Christ' and humbly bowed
Her head for blessing from the saintly man.
She scanned with reverence his features well,
His noble brow and his keen friendly eye,
And then in modesty cast down her look.
In humble spirit she unfurled to him
Her whole life's history, that he might judge,
And then bring light and consolation too
Into her suffering and stricken heart.
She blushed, however, when she had to speak
Of her Fernando, lowering her voice;
But what she came for was the dream itself,
Which like a mystery o'erclouding hung,
Whose deep intent she could not understand.

Now Father Coelestine had listened well
And more than once his eyes had filled with tears,
But drying them he moved his lips in pray'r,
As slowly she before him spread the dream.
He beamed with radiant joy and kindly said:
Dear Soul! be strong and comforted, for sure
Our God has shown great mercy to your soul,
And your own husband will return to grace
And with this holy blessing will return.
I must not tell you more, for so God wills,
But come whene'er your heart depressèd feels

That I may cheer and help to comfort it.
Alwilda, lovely Maiden! with delight
I noticed her and all her virtues true.
And oh! how oft I wished to question her
About you and to bring you to this place.
I feared howe'er temptation thus to cause,
For from a single thought there cometh pride,
Which like a worm destroys the lucious plant.
Now God has brought you here, hence be assured
Of his good grace; and bravely all accept,
Which in his Providence he may impose;
Your crown will all the brighter be, and ah!
How happy, if I could exchange with you.
But pray, as I am feeble, bend and old,
That God his mercy may bestow on me;
Receive my blessing, 'tis our Saviours own,
T'will give you strength and comfort and good
            peace.

And bidding her to follow, showed the way
Through his apartments and the library.
And there displayed his books of deepest thought
In ev'ry field of lit'rature and art,
With gentle touch the pages turning o'er
And having some sweet words at ev'ry turn.
But whilst at illustration's grand effect
He waxed excited in enthusiasm.
His voice grew mellow and his heart dissolved

In love's peculiar feeling, when he reached
For "Martyrs Acts," in which recorded were
What these had suffered for their faith
And for which they enjoy eternal bliss.
Of some he spoke more passingly, but dwelt
Upon the mother of the Machabees
At length, explaining how her seven boys
From oldest down to youngest martyred were;
And when this youngest, only seven years
Of age, his death for Jesus was to meet,
The mother far from trying to dissuade,
Exhorted him to persevere and think
Of that reward, which was awaiting him.

Ah! Peregrina was so happy now
And wished herself a martyr saint to be;
She thanked sincerely Father Coelestine
For all the consolation she received
And hurried home. Alwilda seeing her
Ran out to meet her in her lovely way.
It was a night of true coelestial joy,
When Peregrina told her daughter all
She saw and what the priest of martyr's said,
And then concluded giving thanks to God.

The Village School.

OF all the gifts with which man is endowed,
   There's none so great as mind and intellect,
With which God crowned him as creation's Lord,
That every creature would his servant be.
God, infinitely holy, just and true,
Had necessarily this one intent,
That man to his ideas would conform,
And hence an image and a likeness too
To his own self he had created him.
He pressed the imprint of his godly love
And of his wisdom, deep on Adam's mind,
For which he asked but one obedience,
And showed and drew attention to the fact,
That blessing, peace and happiness must come
Where he's the only object of man's strife ;
And that of all the punishments, this one
The greatest is, to know the good and bad,
Which knowledge satan strongly advertised,
As his idea of a promised deity.
We know that Eve and Adam foolishly
Believed the serpent's mean deceitful word

And as result they learned then to discern
Between the two extremes; but knowledge mean
To choose the bad in ev'ry instance then,
Because by disobeying God, they went
To follow satan, who, you will admit,
Could not, and if he wanted, holy be,
Nor of his subjects sanctity permit.

Thus man had fallen from God's holy grace
Into the devil's piercing, clinching prongs,
From which there was no possible escape
Except that God delivered us from him.
God in his boundless mercy did redeem
Us from the enemy's malicious hold;
But still the greatest gift, which God bestowed
On man, to know but good alone, is lost
And costs the very life-blood to regain,
For only in God's heaven will it be
That of all evil we'll be ignorant.
Yea more! the evil we will easy learn
Without a teacher, whilst obedience
To God is difficult to comprehend,
Although the teachers are so numerous
And in ability rank 'way on top.
There is the conscience, God's loud-speaking voice
Then the comandments written on a stone;
There are the patriarchs, the prophets too,
And Jesus with his holy messengers;

The church which he established firm and true,
Which teaches constantly and never tires,
Assisting even with the sacraments;
When illustrations of all kinds are shown
By all the saints, true servants of the Lord;
Now add to these the visitations all
Wherewith our Father, God! instructeth us:
And, could you say: 'tis easy to be good?

But who is good? This question Jesus placed
And answering himself he said: none is good
Except my Father who in heaven is!
We know his definition to be true,
For absolutely taken God's the source
From which all good it's origin must take :
'S for the good, that we created are
And to obtain the perfect good we live :
All passing things must serve no other end
And perfect wisdom is herein contained.
Because all happiness is rooted here
The wise man says, that all is vanity
And trouble of the spirit, save God's love,
For this alone forever happy makes.

When God had made the world, he saw a need
Of teaching man the use of language too,
But by the parents children must be taught,
And ev'ry child it's mother understands.

The human race, a single family,
Enjoins on men commingled to become.
And as with age the people multiplied,
The teachings of the mothers varied much;
But when, to punish, God confused their tongu
At Babylon's great show of human pride.
Then came necessity the schools to build
In which to learn to speak in such a way
That ev'rybody could his thoughts impart
And, he to whom imparted, understand.
It is apparent how with markings small
Man, when he could not speak, would mark h
                thoughts,
Whence picture-writing was in daily use
Until it was replaced by simpler form.
Now with the words and writing down of sau
The figures went the same progressive way.
Thoughts generated thoughts, and we posess
The fruit of study of all ages past;
This is the way how science came to be
Developed from man's own necessity.
In ev ry branch of learning this is true,
As true it is in ev'ry single art;
What ornaments the single branches have,
They are but outgrowths of convenience.
Now, would we never loose this out of sight,
We'd never fail to know to serve our God.
As science cannot hold beyond the grave:

So relatively taken, all is good,
But absolutely, only love of God.

Look at it as we may, we are compelled
To take recourse to learning, if we want
To gain the joys, which God prepared for us ;
And as by his decree, eternal bliss
Must be acquired whilst here on earth we stay,
Which very stay on earth demands our care,
And study lessens and reduces this,
Therefore we all have gone to school and go.
But of the schools however grand they be
Not one can satisfy, unless it first
And chiefly teaches us the will of God.
It matters not how grand the building is,
Nor if it's name is heralded abroad ;
If only it does truly do its work
To educate the heart and then the mind.

You, Ernest, still remember the oak tree,
The oldest in the place, 'round which we roamed
And on whose branches oft we sat and sang
Or in whose shade we rolling much enjoyed ;
How often lying on our backs we looked
And listened to the merry birdlings' song,
It still holds sway and overshadows well
The old frame school-house, where we used to sit
And vex the teacher with our youthful pranks;

We meant no harm and soon made up for it
By being good and carrying the coal.
It comes to me so often, when at three
The teacher left to get a bite to eat
Whilst we in hunger had to wait till four:
Lest we be noisy during his stay out,
He made you monitor to watch o'er us.
Our friendship then was great, as great as now
And wishing me to please, you asked me soft,
If I would have a certain boy get whipped.
I was surprised, but nodded with my head;
And when the teacher came you him informed
To use the stick, but though you pointed well
My own bad conscience made him turn to me.
With frightened heart you rightened his mistake,
Which after all was right by God's decree.
The same old building you would recognize
With its one spacious room and well worn floor,
The ancient benches having several cuts
And names to tell that others followed us.
The wood is just as hard as once it was,
Though smoothened more by rubbing to and fro;
The hard stone blackboards still are found in place,
With newer scratches scratched and holes worked in
With such a work as makes the boy feel great.
It's all the same to-day; the teacher too
Has his old ways and only with his age
His patience did not keep a lively pace.

And yet we loved him then and thank him now,
As it was better that he was severe.
But boys are boys, it makes me often laugh,
How we would cheat the non-suspecting man;
However, you'll agree, that thanks we owe
Him for the interest he took in us.

* * *

The losing of their home was very hard,
Because instead of granting sympathy
The people wrongly judged the stricken ones;
Now, that Alwilda should be somewhat spared
She for some time remained from school,
But when she started she gave ample proof,
That all her time was given to her books,
And with the best she ably held her own.
This made the children jealous and at once
The evil spirit got the upper hand
Of even those, who always pious were.
For peace, Alwilda had to sit alone
And on the playground none would play with her,
Whilst in small knots they'd stand and talk of her.
You are surprised, that she was left to go
To school amid such circumstances hard;
Nor would it have occured, if she had said
A single word of how they treated her;

But no. she prayed confiding all to God
And offered it for her dear Fathers' soul ;
Moreover, is was her communion year
And suffering helps to prepare for grace.

The Village Church.

GOD has, as we have seen, instructed us
    Through many means, although the truth's but one;
But when his Only Son from heaven came
To teach us all, what we must know and do,
In order to be saved, he summoned twelve,
Whom he apostles called and authorized,
To teach in his own stead the saving Faith.
He gave them all the powers, which he had,
And which were necessary for the soul's
True happiness in this and the next world.
He ordered them to preach and to baptize
And the baptized to strengthen in their faith,
And sins forgive or even to retain;
He asked them to remember his sad death
By changing bread and wine into himself,
And wanted ev'ryone to eat his Flesh
And drink his Blood, for which he promised life;
Providing for conditions, that arise,
He gave us Extreme Unction, Orders too,
And Matrimony for respective ones.

He placed Saint Peter over all the rest,
Which others had disciples under them,
Assisting in the guidance of the flock.
This flock is called the church, with which our Lord
Has promised to remain unto the end.

Rooms soon were needed, and in Christ's own day
We read of Supper in the Dining-Hall,
And of the Hall in which they gathered were
When Jesus send the Paraclete to them.
Hence nothing could have been more natural,
Than that a house they'd built, where God would
                dwell,
And no expense was e'er considered much,
Which went towards adorning such a home.
Nor was it like in time of Salomon,
Who built, though grand it was, but one such house,
For ev'ry land and ev'ry age since then
Display the noble Temples of our God;
And God is grateful for this hearty proof
Of filial obedience and love,
He blesses here on earth the giving hand,
Whilst in the other world he crowns his saints.

Not only for God's honor must it be,
That temples in palatial style are raised,
As man's own weakness has great need of them.
Our Saviour said: My joy's to live with men.

And in a stable near old Bethelem
Was born, who had not where to lay his head;
The Magi came, three wealthy eastern kings,
And on that stable's floor knelt down to pray:
We'd do it too! how often it would be,
Need not be asked, the answer being plain.

Imbued with all these worthy sentiments
From earliest childhood, Father Coelestine
Endeavored with all efforts to adorn
The House of God, as would, considering
Man's inabilities, become our Lord.

The people with harmonious accord
Desired instinctively the very same,
But when it came to bring a sacrifice,
Then few were left, who faithful stood by him.
He toiled and worked and has succeeded well,
But no one would surmise, how difficult
And with what sufferings he pushed ahead.
The very ones, who could have helped the most,
Among the first to want the work well done,
Were nowhere to be found, except it was
To criticize the work in all details;
Now, like the Jews, who treated Jesus mean,
Declared that by the prince of devils he
The devil drove from the possessèd one;
So too of impure motives they accused

The good and zealous Father Coelestine.
Undaunted, he o'ercame each obstacle,
Confiding in the strength from God above.
And now you can behold an edifice
In which the people truly love to stay,
Whilst Jesus in their midst loves to remain,
Inviting all, who heavy burdened are,
To be refreshed at this his fount of love.

T'was here, where Peregrina loved to rest
And open up her heart to our sweet Lord;
With kindest love her look did dwell
Upon the tabernacle's gilded door,
Behind which, she our Saviour knew to be
In mercy list'ning to her humble pray'r.
From tabernacle she her eyes did turn
To Mary's blessed shrine and then towards
St. Joseph, Foster-Father of the child,
And kindest helper of all troubled ones.
She never left without her peaceful mien
Betraying, that she was consoled by God,
And when she had returned to her lone hut,
She thankfully instilled her love of God
Into Alwilda's good and docile heart.

The Instructions.

WITH greatest joy Alwilda loved to hear
 The church-bells ring and call the faith-
 ful all
To come and pay their homage to their God.
Enamored with the choir, but still, absorbed
In conversation with our Savior dear,
With whom to speak the time seemed much too
 short,
She knelt with bended head and folded hands,
A picture more of angel, than of maid.
So edifying, that for once at last,
The judging neighbors found no fault with her.

Her love of Jesus ev'ry day increased,
As she prepared for Love's great sacrament,
In which the son of man would come to her
And she receive our Lord, as God and man.
Most eagerly she hurried to the church
The last instructions to receive, and oh !
How burning a desire had filled her breast,
Increasing hourly as the time approached.

She counted, counted first the many days
And then the hours, which seemed their time t
    stretch,
But when the last instruction day had come,
You would have thought it was the day itself
For which so anxiously she prayed and sighed.

Her mother knew not, should she let her go,
Because she learned of her child's sufferings,
And still more on account of want of food,
As since the yester's dinner there was none.
Could mother send her child a distance off
Without a supper and a breakfast too?
She'd go to Father Coelestine and there
Explain and surely he would let her pass
Although the last instruction she had missed.
But when Alwilda heard of this, she cried
And cried until her mother gave consent,
Assuring her, that God would gran ther strength
Moved, blessing her dear child, she left her go,
And then Alwilda ran, no! fairly flew
As if by angels she was carried on.
She reached the church just as the good old pries
The steps ascended and God's grace implored
To find the words wherewith he'd fascinate
And fill the children's hearts with humble love,
As love alone can worthily meet love;
Then, having said her prayer, she sat down

And listened most attentively, her gaze
On Father Coelestine's steadfastly fixed.
It seemed as if she fairly drank his words,
Absorbing all their spirit and intent.
The pious children and the good old priest
Could scarce refrain from constant watching her,
Although their own souls filled up to the brim
With love, desire and kindest gratitude
For their sweet Saviour, who would come to them.

Now Father Coelestine, a learned man,
Was Master of the rhetoricians' art,
Besides he knew full well the human soul
And was possessed of greatest warmth in love.
He never rose so high above himself
As when for First Communion he'd prepare
The youthful hearts with meditations grand.
Most certainly, it was the grace of God
Which ev'ry word of his effective made,
But this time more than ever he was raised,
Undoubtedly by special grace, and moved
To tears from the beginning to the end.
He ev'ry effort made to picture well
The birth and life and passion of our Lord,
And pleaded strongly with o'erpow'ring plea,
That Joseph, passing Beth'lem's inns, would choose
To enter in their hearts and there prepare
A happy birth-place for the Virgin-child,

That they should promise, never to disturb
The mother's tender care for her sweet-babe,
And that for Jesus they'd prepare a crib
Of gentle love, wherein he'd gladly rest.

His tender words, and great emotion had
The much desired effect and grasped
The hearts of all his faithful listeners.
But when he spoke of Gods own mother dear,
He paused at once and motionlessly stood,
With eyes and hands toward Alwilda turned;
The children too were looking fixed at her.
No wonder! her love rose to such degree,
That in bright beams the beauty of the soul
Showed through the mortal body, white as snow;
And rising in the air some sev'ral feet,
She seemed to kneel on clouds of brightest light.
The priest, no doubt inspired, walked down to he
And whispered soft: Alwilda — pray for me.
At once returned, — she blushed and worried mucl
As she had done, when, her two dreams she told
And feared an angel's secret was betrayed.
Instructions over, Father Coelestine
Gave out the word, that none should question her
And she herself confided it to none.

Now out into the streets and far and wide
The news like lightning quickly had been spread:

saint! a saint! was heard on ev'ry hand
nd in the hearts the resolution formed
o see the saint the coming holyday.

The Happiest Day.

THE ev'ning sun in brightest garment set
    And quiet took possession of the town;
The revellers for once remained at home
Most anxiously inquiring of what they
Had heard and which engaged the minds of all,
What at the last instruction had occured.
Fernando brought the news to his good wife,
Who doubted and kept doubting of the truth
Because Alwilda had not mentioned it.
Far from the thought, that it could be her child.
She still would not reproach and hence delayed
To place the question to her daughter dear;
But yet! discard it as she may, it came
E er back to her till she could scarcely wait
For break of dawn, when surely it would out.

She felt so happy, when Alwilda came,
Because God helped her to a goodly price,
For a rich dress, which she had brought with he
But which she never wore since that sad day
When she was driven out from house and home.
It entered not her mind, that the proceeds

Might soon be gone, but trusting in her God
Prepared a meal, the like they did not have,
Since in the lonely hut they entered in.

The day is come and with the break of light
From far surrounding country people flocked
With fleety feet and vehicles so fleet
As if an all-depending race they ran.
They headed for the Village-Church, whose bells
Rang out their festive lay in glad appeal
For all to come and worship here their Lord.

The children, gathered in the Village-School,
Were dressed by dext'rous hands with wreath and
                       veil,
And good Alwilda was so much rejoiced,
Because enabled to refund the same.
The priest, surprised, yet did not dare to ask:
Whence came the blessing? whence she came to
                       this?
But in his heart had offered thanks to God
And wondered at his mercy, love and care.

The priest in surplice and biretta came,
Preceded by the Cross and Altar-Boys,
Who on this festive day their best had dressed,—
To lead the way and bring as offering
His children good before the Holy Lord.

The people stood, some on the street, some climbed
The trees and fences for a better view,
And when the children came the necks were craned
And eyes were eager scanning ev'ryone,
At last in spite of veil and bended head
Alwilda's sainted face was recognized;
A stir went through the crowd, a whisper heard!
Alwilda blushed and quickly signed herself:
A ray of light flashed from her holy brow,
But all absorbed she was disturbed no more.

The children in the church, the people too!
The house of God was filled as ne'er before.
It was a joy to see how single soul
A thousand brings before the throne of God,
Whom often no consideration moves
To pay their tribute to the Mighty One.

The song and music, far from frivolous,
Was this time pious, humble, soul-inspiring too;
And Father Coelestine had oft to pause,
His soul enwrapt in contemplating God,
And when his last address he humbly held,
No eye was dry and hardened sinners wept,
Save one who restless moved in non-control
When the good priest had asked the children all
To not forget their parents in their pray'r
When Jesus, their sweet God, shall come to them.

The holy sacrifice was offered so
As ever it should be by God's command
And as Almighty God does well deserve,
But which we often grow forgetful of,
Thus treating careless this God-given work.

The children seem quite pale and weak and sick,
Not from the lengthened fast, but from their love's
intensity and burning of desire,
But are refreshed as Altar boys now ring:
The time has come, when Jesus comes to them.
And slowly two by two, with downcast eyes,
Their hands so lightly folded, now they go,
Escorted by the whole celestial court,
And genuflect so humbly and ascend
The Altar steps, where lovingly they wait.
More humble still than e'er before, the priest
With Jesus in his hand to show to all
His "Dominus non sum dignus" thrice repeats,
To which 'O Lord I am not worthy' they
Most humbly, as becoming answer give.
Then promising eternal life to them
He modestly lays Jesus on their tongue,
That they shall henceforth be 'another Christ.'

The children were so happy, angel-like,
As they returned, that all were edified
And envied them their truly godly bliss.

Alwilda was the last one to receive
And ev'ry eye was firmly fixed on her;
Herself, she knew but Jesus all alone
And in her heart she left none other in.

She wore an Angel's smile in stepping down
But was so pale, that people whispered low,
And made a stir to go assisting her,
When, near the lowest step, she paused and knelt,
And bowing somewhat prayed most earnestly.
A halo now appeared of dusky light
But gradually brightened more and more
Until it was so bright, as bright can be;
And as the brightness brightened she was seen
To sink down lower,—lower then she dropped!
Her spotless soul to God above had flown.

The faithful held their breath, the priest went on
The sacrifice to end; again a stir,
A thought and pray'r of sympathy, when now
Sad Peregrina to the Altar fled
And with the gentlest care Alwilda raised
And, in her arms embrace, her carried home.
No tongue can tell the sorrow of her heart,
And yet, she was consoled; Alwilda came
In spirit back, her blessing to bestow.
As she was carried by the people pray'd,
A blessing to receive and gently touched

he holy relic of Alwilda's corpse;
ut! suddenly they turned and looked around
o see the one, who here could sighing be
'here all gave praise and thanks to God.
ernando never knew it was his child
ntil as corpse his wife her carried by,
nd then endeavoring to follow her
)uld not succeed, though thrice he did attempt.
e made his peace with God and most contrite
e humbly to the priest his sins confessed,
nd since that day, ne'er better man there was.

Conclusion.

DEAR Ernest, be not saddened o'er death,
Whose hand and heart you came so far to woe;
Think not, that God has tried Alwilda hard,
For happier lot could never have been her's,
Nor brighter crown be placed upon her head!

She is a martyr! offering her life
For the salvation of her father's soul.
When she her dreams to Peregrina told,
She told not all, and fearing that she did,
She worried, lest a secret she betrayed;
When she had pray'd and her good Angel said
The day of his conversion would yet come,
He asked her first to bring a sacrifice
And she at once had begged to give her life,
Accepting which the Angel said: Amen!

You never could have loved her any more
Than her dear sainted mother always did,
And now loves more, and yet she'd be the last

call her back from her eternal bliss,
could Alwilda make her happier,
he'd return; for all's entirely changed
l they are blessed and honored more
in in the days gone by they ever were;
l though 'twas sad, they with bold letters wrote:

s was the day which God in mercy made!
l hence with joy we praise his holy name,
o called Alwilda to his happy home
l brought Fernando back to peace and love.
l shedding blessing on the lowly hut;
erefore good Peregrina gratefully
: praises sings of that Communion Day.

A CHRISTMAS CAROL.

Christmas Eve.

HAVE all the children gone to bed,
    And are they fast asleep?
Then see, that you will make no noise,
And on your toes now creep;
Yea! whisper only when you speak
And lose no time at all,
For very late it grew to be,
Ere they to sleep did fall.

Bring here the painted wooden stand,
Which rails and posts surround,
Whilst I will get the mighty tree,
So nice and full around;
I'll taper now its solid stem
And wedge it in the hole:
Ah! what a pleasure and delight
They'll have, upon my soul!

Come, hang the Angel 'way on top,
His Gloria we will sing,
That he may grant to us the peace
Of Christ, the new-born King;
Hang here and there a tapering nut,
Quite dazzling bright and gay,
And sometimes bunch them in a group,
And turn them more this way.

Suspend some apples in between,
You know the children's taste,
Besides the yellow, green and red
Will take the eye with haste;
To sweeten more the pleasant sight,
The finest candy bring,
Of various colors and of shapes,
That fetch the laughter's ring.

Bring on the many fancy cakes
Of Brownie's comic style,
Whereas the ornaments of tin
I will attach the while;
Then wind the branches all around
With fringe of golden hue,
And sometimes mix some silver in
With green and pink and blue.

The candles stand a distance off,
And bring the isin-glass,
Hang many pieces all around,
To mirror candles'-mass;
Below you put the clown and bear,
The cub and lioness,
Some sheep and also shepherd dogs
And things I cannot guess.

A monkey with his turning pole,
A comic music box,
A mule with rugged rope for tail
And that fierce-looking ox; —
Then over here you put the gun.
Tin soldiers with their swords,
A locomotive and a throng
Of children's festive sports.

The sled and skates are here in place
Aside a cabinet box
With hatchet, saw and rule and square
And many building blocks.
The newest clothes pile very high,
Whereever there is room;
And place a washtub near to them
And next to this a broom;

A kitchen with its tiny stove,
And many dishes too,
For little children take delight
In finding work to do;
But for their recreation give
Them dolls in gayest dress
And little baby carriages,
And they'll not cease to bless.

Stop grumbling! for the bill you've made
Is more than overpaid,
In grateful feelings of the young
In life, both soon and late;
Moreover, when you're old you'll love
To see the very same,
For your own joy and comfort too;
So do not, pray! complain.

Take off your shoes and sneak up stairs,
And softly 'waken them,
Then sing to them the happy hymn
Which Angels sang for them;
And tell them how good Santa Claus
Had been so kind to all,
That down the chimney he had come,
But went out through the hall.

And when he on the threshhold stood,
Before he hurried home,
He said, that of their sweets they should
Give to the poorer some.
He lightly jumped into his sleigh,
The sack upon his back,
And blowed so strong into his horn
And gave the deers a whack.

So bring them hither to the tree,
The candles are all lit,
And let them look at everything
And taste of every bit,
Whilst we from out their open eyes
Their happy feelings read,
Receiving thus their grateful love,
The truest Christmas treat.

Christmas Morning.

I HEAR the bells' sweet ringing,
　There's music in the air;
They peal so sweet and lofty,
They ring so clear and fair;
And far into the darkness
Unto the greeting light,
They call the wandering pilgrim
To come to church this night.

The ground has dressed its whitest,
The virgin snow, untrod,
And from an azure heaven
The stars already shot,
Continuing their shooting
To show their happy joy,
Whilst atmosphere surrounds us,
As spirits would enjoy.

From out a peaceful slumber
Arises all mankind,
And 'mid a whispering stillness
Men shroud their peaceful mind.
The fathers and the mothers
And children good and sweet,
Are making ready quickly
Their holy Love to greet.

The animals are astirring
And feel so fresh and gay,
As if they had a knowledge
Of this great night and day,
With silvery bells atinkling,
They lightly trod the ground,
And, with their measured stepping,
Create a pleasant sound.

The bells have rung their pealing,
And chimes have followed then,
And hearts are with them rhyming,
In mountain home or glen,
Devoutest greeting Anthems
For him, who dwells on high,
Who deigned to come among us
To be to us so nigh.

Ah! how the organ swelleth,
So proud in happy glee,
To tell the chant of Angels
In sweetest harmony:
Oh! Gloria in excelsis
To God, to God it be!
And peace to men of good-will,
So happy and so free!

Oh! Gloria in excelsis,
To God, who pitied us,
To men of grateful feelings,
Who ever love him thus;
Oh! Gloria in excelsis,
To God becoming man,
To all his peace is promised,
If they but to him ran!

And in a little manger
There lieth a sweet child,
In swaddling clothes enwrappèd,
It looks so sweet and mild;
Its eyes bespeak affection,
It begs us to come near,
And in its earnest pleading
It seems to shed a tear.

Its little lips encourage,
As if they beg a kiss,
And in return their breathing
Will then bestow a bliss;
Its little arms so loving
Extend to call us nigh,
In love they would embrace us,
That heart to heart may sigh.

And oh! what glad rejoicing
Would fill that loving heart,
If, to each other clinging,
We never more would part. —
Behind it kneels the mother,
In piety so mild,
With mother's joy and feeling
Upon her new-born child.

And yet! she holds it pleading,
That we it should embrace,
And grant to her the kindness
To kiss its lovely face;
Yea, more! she begs in earnest,
That we would ever grant.
To hold it in our memory,
As we would in our hand.

But ah! she weeps and sadness
O'er shades her noble brow,
Foreseeing in her spirit,
How we to hatred bow. —
A man stands there uncovered
In deepest prayer staid,
His eyes rest on the baby,
There in the manger laid.

So eloquent a silence,
As his, was never seen;
Oh! that we could declare it,
Here has our model been. —
On either side apeeping,
There is an ox and ass,
Who, in their simple feeling,
Love here their time to pass:

For oh! this sweetest baby,
Whom would it not have brought,
When even holy kings have
Its humble crib besought!
They knelt down in this stable,
Upon the nakèd floor,
Whilst we, oh we! too noble!
Remain but at the door.

The shepherds too! but of these,
It surely was but right,
But why are we not like them,
To feel like them aright? —
This child, this child! who is it?
Who else, but our great God?
Who on the cross will suffer,
And once decide our lot,

When on the day of judgement
He'll come with splendor bright,
Yea, brighter far than ever
Has brightness been this night.
When heaven's gates flew open
And Angels did appear
And gave their happy tidings
And told them not to fear;

They sang so sweet, that ages
Have never tired to sing,
The song, that brought rejoicings
And blessings e'er will bring.

    Gloria in excelsis,
    Let the Anthem sound,
    In excelsis Deo
    From hill to valley bound!

Gloria in excelsis,
To our new-born king,
In excelsis Deo,
All the nations sing!

Gloria in excelsis,
To the Virgin Queen,
In excelsis Deo,
Who her child has been!

Gloria in excelsis,
To St. Joseph too;
In excelsis Deo,
Best of servants true!

Gloria in excelsis,
To the angel throng;
In excelsis Deo,
Roll the song along!

Gloria in excelsis,
To the young and old;
In excelsis Deo,
As by angels told!

Pax hominibus,
Men of sterling worth;
Bonae voluntatis,
Over all the earth!

So may a merry christmas
Come to one and all;
We love its sweetest echo,
Rebounding from the stall.

No greater joy could ever
Be granted by our Lord,
Than he has granted to us,
When Flesh was made the Word.

Hence, Glory in the Highest,
To our new-born King,
To our sweetest Baby
Let the Anthem Ring!

Christmas Day.

THE people are athronging,
   From out the temple's door,
Where they had been adoring
Bend low on clean-washed floor;
Abounding with all graces,
Which God so kind bestowed,
They proved the Angel's wishes,
Which from his lips had flowed

In strains so elevating,
So sweet and lovely too,
Of Glory to our Saviour
And Peace to all men true;
And from this peace is leaping,
With all o er bounding haste,
That love, which binds together,
And which all nations praised.

Hence hand the hand is taking,
And lip to lip descends,
As with a 'Merry Christmas'
The one to other bends;
Then little cups are giving
Such happy christmas joys,
For Grand Pa and Grand Mother,
And for the girls and boys.

But who can tell the pleasure
Which parents this day have?
As they enjoy so sweetly
To see their young ones laugh.
Now in their overflowing
With wishes and with love,
They would have sheer forgotten
To mind the kitchen stove.

This patiently was waiting
To be of service too,
Since if the stomach's empty,
Enjoyments are but few;
The mother therefore hurries
And rakes the fire well,
To add the pleasant flavor
Of bracing kitchen-smell.

She exits to the pantry
And brings a mighty goose,
Which she had long been fattening
And fretted much to lose;
The goose had grown so heavy,
Yes, even after death!
That all her strength was needed
To fetch it in, they said.

Still, she was very lucky,
And did not leave it fall,
And pushed it in the oven,
And seemed so proud and tall.
She poured some water to it,
So it would not be burned,
Then mixed the finest gravy,
As she had 'specially learned.

She mashed potatoes quickly,
And made the apple-sauce,
Then spread with cloth the table
And pulled it straigth with force,
The dishes placed in order,
And silver forks and knives
She said, the best is wanted
This day by all housewifes.

When all was done, she signalled,
And each one took his chair;
The father first in order,
Then boys and maidens fair.
Down to the little youngster,
Who could not bide his time,
Till he was helped to cutlings
And pounded forth a chime.

And when at last a little
Was put upon his plate,
It tasted, oh! so sweetly,
He could no longer wait,
Until some more was given
He licked his spoon the while;
But soon his wait was over
And he began to smile.

They all enjoyed it richly,
The quiet father said;
It was the best he tasted,
Such taste he never met!
With lightest heart the mother
Rid off the table quick,
And brought the blessèd pudding,
Which looked so very slick;

Next pies of mellow apples,
And cakes of every kind
With nuts and fruits and candies
And things I cannot mind.
Ah! they had sure a dinner,
They will not soon forget!
Their cheeks were swollen greatly,
Their eyes were very red.

Now after this the coffee,
So sweet and hot was brought,
Which all enjoyed in quaffing
And then a rest besought.
Devoutly saying Graces,
They left the table glad,
But still a trifle heavy,
Perhaps a little sad.

They knew not just the wherefore,
But we with sober mind
Remember, that the stomach,
When filled the heart does bind;
More quiet than expected,
Perhaps in rest and sleep,
The afternoon was spending
And night came on a creep.

The supper was a light one
And so the evening came
With far a better feeling
And worthy of the name,
Because the family gathered
Around the fireside,
In circle as they called it,
Whose half was not in sight.

Once more admitting freely
The goose was very good,
They claimed, they still were tasting
This richest of all food.
Yet one thing gave rejoicing,
And sure it was the goose!
As they remembered Martha,
Of whom they had got news:

That she was old and feeble,
And could not go outdoor,
Nor could she send for goodies,
As she was much too poor;
So they brought her a portion,
And brought it with good will,
And begged her to enjoy it,
Together with its fill.

So now they studied over
How glad she must have been,
When, without expectation,
They had come on the scene;
This made them very happy,
E'en when the day had fled,
That they resolved in future
Poor never to forget.

Christmas Night.

THE evening was so quiet,
The Air a gentle breeze,
But streets were all vacated;
They were much like the fleece
Of cotton, when in blossom,
As o'er the little place
The moon was slow ascending
With always brighter face.

The trees threw living shadows,
More spectre-like than e'er,
And all together quiet
The night was everywhere,
But such a lovely heaven
Was long again unseen,
Since stars so bright were shining,
The like had seldom been.

Occasionally footsteps
Resounded cracking snow;—
As if of one in hurry,
With spirits rather low,
Because his wife was lying
On sickness' hardened bed,
And he still hoped the doctor
Would stop her early death.

Perhaps it was with gladness,
He trod the covered earth
With happy speculation
Upon the offspring's worth.
Again there comes a footstep,
Irregular and stiff,
Which sounds, as if it's going
Toward a dangerous cliff;

For clearly it reboundeth
At sight of every tree,
From every moving shadow,
From every thing, that be;
The moon feels sore offended
And draws her face to frown,
And shakes her head momentous,
As she is looking down.

The earth next loses balance
And seems to leave its hold,
And trees are leaning forward,
So daring and so bold,
That this poor pilgrim loseth
The presence of his mind,
And cannot bear it longer,
Nor can he foothold find!

Despairing, he outreaches
To catch a fence nearby,
When even this recedeth
And from him seems to fly;
A big tree seemed aleaning
Toward him for an aid,
But as he wished to grasp it,
It would no longer wait.

Then perfectly discouraged,
He made a mighty jump,
But missed the wished-for-object
And falls all in a lump;
He tried and tried to get up
And rolled upon his back,
His hands and feet were upward,
A shapeless bundled sack:

His eyes were rolling wildly,
In Tremens' horrid proof,
When ah! the bells were tinkling
And came the sound of hoof.
The children in their weeping,
The mother in her tears!
They stopped the brisky horses
And brought some carrying biers;

Then, having rolled him on them,
They shoved him in the sleigh,
And cut the horses sharply
And hurried on their way. —
Another footstep lighty,
Has passed the kitchen door,
The father heard it faintly
And quickly paced the floor.

He reached the window timely
To see a youth pass by,
Whose hat was down his forehead;
He hurried on a fly,
And yet he sought the shadows,
Avoiding every light,
Until he seemed to vanish
Into the darkened night.

But ah! his soul much darker
This Holy Night knew not,
And what a sad affliction
Awaiteth him from God,
Who from his little manger
Has followed him with eyes,
First pleading, then in anger
For living in such-wise!

Then offering a prayer,
That none may come to grief,
The father left the window
And felt a great relief,
To see the family circle,
So happy and so gay,
With peace upon their foreheads
And fairylike a fay.

The children kindly begged him
To tell a story nice,
As he had oftened promised,
But left it in that wise;
This time, it being Christmas,
He would not put them off,
And waited but their asking,
As he held them in love.

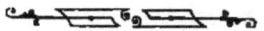

Then bringing in a heavy log,
He put it on the fire,
And drew his chair a little near,
And asked them not to tire,
For it would take a little while
Before he would be through
With what he was to tell them now,
A story good and true.

When man had fallen from his God,
God's mercy did not fly,
But promised him a Saviour then,
If good to be he'd try;
And many years had passed away
Before the Saviour came,
Who was the one desired by all
And Jesus was his name.

You've heard of his most glorious birth,
Though in a stable 'twas,
Whose Angels told it to the world,
Whose Star had guided us;
And when this Jesus grew in years,
He thought all how to live,
If they would care the great reward
Of Heaven to receive.

But many, who had heard him speak,
And saw his godly deeds,
Refused in malice to believe
And followed passion's heats,
They falsely persecuted him,
Yes, nailed him to the cross,
But having risen from the dead,
He suffered hence no loss.

Yea, rather in this very way,
He saved us from that death,
From which to save us he had come
And spent his every breath!
Now from that moment it was plain,
There is one only way,
Which leads to heaven's bliss above,
'Tis by the cross, they say!

And so the followers of Christ
Have all had much to bear,
So much indeed, that it would make
All fill with utmost fear,
Were it not for the simple fact,
That heaven's worth it all,
And that our God will never try,
To make us really fall;

For he will grant enormous grace,
Supporting us with might,
And hence we find the saints so glad,
A model for our sight;
Besides, if we ne'er overlook,
That life must pass away,
And far beyond this world we look,
We'd wish with saints to stay.

'Though hard and harder they are tried,
With sufferings unkind,
It is just in this very way,
They greater glory find!
The story which I now relate,
Is sad enough to thrill
The souls of even hardened one's.
And eyes with tears to fill.

And yet, when all I shall have said,
I know you'll gladly say,
If only you could be with them.
Of whom I speak to-day.

The days of Rome, the Empire great,
Were quickly closing down,
As it no longer boasted of
Its Generals with renown,
Save now and then a lonely star,
Whose light would soon die out,
Since death with most unsparing hand,
Prepares for each a shroud.

But whilst such hero would yet live,
We easily perceive,
He'd hold esteem within his grasp
And honored love receive,
Just such a one our hero was,
Called Placidus by name,
Who by his friendliness as well,
Deserved his bravery's fame.

For all his stalward soldiers said:
'A Father! truly he,
'And kinder General ne'er had been,
'Nor could there ever be!'
Like all the Generals of old,
He very rich had grown,
And many were the Slaves he held,
And Stock and Land he'd own.

Enjoying life, as all would do,
Who boast of wealth and friends,
He often had his feast-day-outs
And sought the deer in rents;
And so he chanced one day to see
A precious specimen,
And in persuit he charged his steed,
Behind him all his men.

Soon over brush and over logs,
That covered thick the ground,
The steed of purest blood had flown,
And further onward bound,
The followers soon lacked behind,
Nor could they understand
That charger's swiftest passing on
As if on magic wand.

When far into the deepest wood,
Where all was still as death,
The deer had turned and faced him,
From whom it so far fled.
Immediately a cross appeared
Between its Antlers great,
A cross of brightest golden hue,
And then a voice had said:

'Why persecutest, Placidus,
Thou me, who loved thee so?'
And thereupon our General asked,
'Ah! where bidst thou me go?'
I know not all, that passed between,
The General and our Lord,
But this I know, that he was now,
Converted by God's word.

For three long days the wood was searched,
But search was all in vain,
Despairing then of finding him,
They came, a saddened train;
But quietly himself had come,
A different man was he,
And greeting his dear loving wife,
He showed, what life should be,

Explaining all that he had seen,
And what he had been told,
Inducing her to go with him
Into Faith's happy fold.
The pope himself instructed them
With illustrations grand,
And showed them, that to suffer here,
Meant gaining Heaven's land;

He told them what great happiness
Was held for them in store,
But that it also would be hard,
What they must bear before.
Prophetic were the words he spoke,
But then a warrior old
Minds not the crosses of the road,
Nor lurking danger's hold.

With joy, with joy they were baptized
And with them their two boys;
The gladdest joys came o er the church,
And God increased these joys.
God's holy consolations have
At all times given strength
To every resolution good
And for duration's length;

And hence the days of Placidus
Were piously bespent
At home or in the Catacombs,
Where every night he went
With Theopista, his good wife,
And with his children all,
Called Agapitus, older boy,
And Theopistus, small.

My kingdom is not of this world,
Says Christ our Lord and King;
And hence you cannot here expect
To hear but angels sing.
Another world, it is above,
Alone can grant reward,
But this reward must here be earned,
Though it be e'er so hard.

Not long, not long was joy to rule
Our hero's noble heart,
For soon affliction came o'er him
And stinging was its smart.
A fearful hail-storm o'er his crops
Destroyed what he had raised,
But he had learned to bear it well,
And hence God's name he praised;

Then sickness decimated swift
And carried off his stock,
But also this he bravely bore
And bore without a shock.
But when the people had surmised, —
Because he kept aloof,
From all the pagan services,
And this was surely proof! —

That he must be a christian now,
Then he bethought himself,
Concluding to depart from Rome
Unto some distant delve.
Say not, that he a coward was,
Who thought of his good wife
And of his little children dear,
So young yet in their life.

Then selling what to him remained,
It was so very wee,
He set out for far Nubia,
More quiet rest to see.
In going he a river met,
Which flowed so wild and strong,
That he then bargained for a boat
To carry them along

To any nearest landing place,
And his good price he paid;
But when the ship was turnèd in
The harbor's landing gate,
The captain held on to the wife
And asked for heavy fee
Of ransom ere he'd let her go;
Demanding greater fee

Than Placidus could ever pay,
Who begged and pleaded so;
But all, alas! was of no use,
As he was made to go.
The real reason for this deed
Was wicked sinful lust,
And hence our hero felt it worse
And yet in God he'd trust!

Now Theopista prayed and wept,
And God had heard her too!
For soon the captain was convinced,
She'd die! ere be untrue
To him, whom God had given her,
And who so kind had been;
Now that, she even was baptized,
Ah! no, she'd never sin!

But Placidus his name had changed
In baptism to Eustace,
And so we must from henceforth put
Him in his christian place.
Now having offered all to God
He travelled with his boys
Far over hills and deserts wild
To give them better joys.

Again a stream, but not a boat
To carry them across,
Nor could he venture both to take
Without a fear of loss.
He placed the one upon the ground,
The other in his arm;
And plied with mighty force the stream.
Which brought him so much harm.

Scarce had he reached the farther shore,
When suddenly a cry
Had come from over yonder there
And wolves were running by.
The little boy was carried off
Far into distant wood,
And Eustace hurried after them
When lo! aghast he stood:

For ah! a lion took with ease
The other in his mouth,
And hurried with him far away,
Whilst Eustace shrieked aloud.
When hardened warriors start to weep
Then talk of suffering pain!
Such was the case right in this wild,
Where Eustace cried in vain;

But, overcoming all his grief,
He saw, the hand of God
Had send all this for his own good,
And hence he'd bear his lot;
Yes like a perfect christian would,
A soldier of our Lord,
Who knows, that he in heaven will
Find all of his own sort.

However with a serious turn
This school of suffering bore
Upon his mind a dreariness,
'Though peace it left in store.
He wandered on, of all bereft,
And took a laboring job,
Upon a farmer's rich estate, —
This veritable Job!

Ah! often was his spirit low,
And often he did weep,
As memories of by-gone times
Would o'er his bosom creep.
How earnest was his pleading then,
Whose very frame would shake,
That heaven should restore to him
For what in sleep he'd wake.

'Yes, God is good, he often said,
'Again he showed his love,
'He spread a vision for my eyes,
'A vision from above:
'In it I met my saintly wife,
'My holy children too,
'And then a voice had told to me:
'This all will once be true.

Again 'I saw us brought before
'The pagan Emperor,
'Our lives to offer to our God,
'And so reach heaven's door.
Then fifteen years he toiled and worked,
And wished for that great day,
When once again his eyes should see
His wife and children gay.

The Romans were engaged in war
And things were much adverse,
And rightly Trajan was afraid,
That matters would grow worse;
He therefore cared to have the man,
Who previously had fought
His battles with successful hand,
And laurels home had brought.

A grand reward he promised those,
Who'd bring this General back;
And hence they sought through all the land,
Till they would find his track.
Two faithful soldiers met him then,
But recognized him not
Till having told their mission and
Inspired by voice of God

He showed the scar upon his head
And asked them, who he was,
When sure they wept, as children would
To meet their General thus.
He laid aside his farming tools
And followed them to Rome,
Where he was placed in high command
In his once glorious home.

Not many weeks had then elapsed
Before his work was done.
He drove the enemy from the field
Back in disordered run.
His heart was big with kindest love,
And 'father' was his name,
As him the soldiers all would call,
Respecting much the same.

Yet, who can help, that similars
Will feel attached and drawn,
Which is but nature's goodly work,
That like to like is borne.
Of all the soldiers there were two
Both young and strong and brave,
So humble too, that Placidus
Them kind attention gave.

They were attached, as friends in need,
And bound themselves by vow,
To help each other at all times
In peace or battle row.
The Roman army planted tents
To rest a day or so,
Ere with great joy it would return
And back to Rome would go.

But these two heroes left the camp
To have a quiet chat,
And were no doubt dejected much,
You ask, but what of that?
The older asked the younger one,
What pressed his heart so much?
And this one told the simple tale,
That any one would touch:

How he was raised by peasants good,
Who saved him from a beast,
But could not find his family,
That they could so be pleased,
Yea more, as sure he noble was,
As his necklace would show,
And hence he often tempted was
To seek both high and low;

But not a rising hope has sprung
To grant him his request,
Wherefore he joined the army then,
Believing death is best.
And now the elder wiped his tears
And looked the locket o'er,
Then hung around the younger's neck
And wept so much the more;

He saw his mother's picture there
And found his brother too,
Then told him how himself had been
Rescued by sheperds true
From out a lion's fearful mouth,
Whilst they were on a chase;
They cared for him in charity
Until he turned his gaze

To find his noble father too
And hoped for it at Rome,
Where they had lived in former days
In fine palatial home.
They rose to tell the General
Their precious, precious find,
When suddenly a voice was heard,
That started from behind;

The enemy had rallied soon
And meant to give surprise,
But oh! these heroes ever brave
Were now no less the wise!
They held the enemy in check
Upon a narrow bridge,
Until the army had come up
And threw them in the ditch.

The battle o'er, the General
Had send for these brave men,
Who saved the army by their pluck,
And send an escort then
To bring them with great honors in;
But they were at the door
To tell the General their great joy
To heighten it the more.

The General listened with surprise,
But soon his eyes were wet,
As they their entire history told
And he his sons here met!
Describe the hearts most noble joy?
'Tis more than I can do!
I can but only feel the same
And you should feel it too;

What God prepared in holy love
All words must fail to tell,
When after all these many years
It ended all so well!
'Twas hard to bear, 'tis surely true!
But ah! this instant great,
Has changed it all to loveliness,
A happy, happier fate!

The following day they struck their camp
And started to return,
With laurels well-deserved, to Rome,
Where incense they should burn.
The headquarters were in a hut,
Which held a woman old,
Who, gray of hair and many griefs,
Owned nothing to be told.

She lived from fishes many years
And what the ground would yield,
But all her life was dreary-like
'Though peace was her great shield.
Before the General left her hut,
She begged an interview
Then told how she had hailed from Rome
And what she suffered too.

She prayed, that he would take her back
To friends most dear to her,
Who surely would give her a home;—
She tried his heart to stir!
No sooner had she spoken all
When Eustace raised his hat,
And showed his scar and asked, if she
Still recognizeth that?

Pray tell me what the feelings were,
When heart to heart was blend ;
Oh! how that vision had come true,
Which such a day had meant!
Ah! in those few and shortened hours,
Who measures all their love?
Who else can do it, save the One,
Who dwelleth up above!

The next day they were on their way,
To martyr-blood-stained Rome,
Where all the populace turned out
To welcome them back home.
But something strange possessed the crowd,
And cautiously they said:
'How can it be? no captives were,
'Whose blood the beasts would get?

'Yea! Placidus did not give thanks,
'To their so famous God';
A God, whom they held in esteem,
But who was worse than naught.
Then very soon they struck a thought,
The thought took vital form,
And hence the senate made demand,
Demand by greatest storm,

That Placidus should sacrifice
The incense as of old,
But he rejoiced to testify
And so his faith he told.
Then Trajan tried a winsome way,
But Eustace faithfully
Held out until his parting breath ;
Likewise the other three !

When seeing all attempts as vain
The Emperor grew mad,
And ordered them then 'to the beasts',
Which made our heroes glad.
But see! the animals so wild,
Became at once so tame,
And though they once had brought distress,
They seemed regretting same.

Then Trajan roared out his command
To 'heat the furnace red
And fill it up with oil, and throw
Them in this awful bed.'
Thus Eustace, Theopista and
His children both were thrown.
Into this boiling oil, to find
Their death without a groan.

Yes, martyrs' crowns bedecked their heads
And palms they held in hand,
When they had passed the earthly shore
Into yon better land!
They're happy now, as they can be,
These seventeen hundred years,
And no more suff'ring 'waiteth them .
And dried are all their tears;

Their names are written in the book,
The book containing life.
And showing what God gives to those,
Who faithfully will strive,
To reach the Heaven he has made
For those, that him will serve
And never dream of doing wrong,
Nor from the right will swerve:

For ah! no eye hath ever seen,
Nor ear hath ever heard,
Nor came it into human heart,
Says the Apostle's word,
What God prepared for those,
That love and serve him true
And persevere unto the end
Amid all conflict too!

———

The father said: This children! is
What I desired to tell,
That you may ere remember it,
And put to practise well,
The faithfulness, which you have seen
In these great Saints of God,
And with them once partake of bliss
And their coelestial lot.

Then mindful, that it grew quite late,
He called them to say grace
To Jesus in his cosy crib,
Whence come all charming rays
Of love and peace for all mankind,
That joy to each may come,
And bliss may hover everywhere
In high or humble home.

With wishes, that next Christmas would
Find them again the same,
He bid them sleep a sweet good night
And blessed them in God's name.

St. Patrick.
Patron of Ireland.

A happy boy is led away, a slave is made of him,
    The parents and the sisters gay their sight with tears made dim;
For oh! the angiush of the heart, as he returned no more.
From bandits and fetters hard, from yonder distant shore.
And daily they went on their knees, and daily sighed and prayed,
And daily they looked o'er the seas; — for his return they wait.
They felt their hope so all forlorn, of him no sign appeared,
They felt the worry by him borne, his very life they feared.

And he, a happy boy, is made a slave in truest deed,
To do the hardest work he's bade;—they lash his back and feet;—
To feed the flock on grassy hill, he's sent out by command
And be the weather as it will, he famished had to stand.
Thus suffering in body much, he had but one Friend near!
And when dejected felt his touch,—the touch of one so dear!
It is his God, who is all-where, and whom he felt so nigh,
Who would this youth so well prepare to lead the souls on high.

At home they restless were, and prayed for God to send him back,
But ah! how long they had to wait, as hope seemed dark and black!

But God is good and in his time will make all things come right,
And after ev'ry winter's clime there comes a summer bright.
He showed the boy in vision's light, that he should flee from hence,
And to the distant shore he hied to find a ship go thence,
Whose crew had forced him back again for want of passage-pay,
But touched by grace had called him then to cross the ocean's way.

For this he preached the living God in thanks for their kind deed,
And deep though slow had taken root the Faith's most wondrous seed.
The voyage was a fearful one, and when they reached a shore, —
Successfully, 'tis true, 'twas done,—they found no food in store.
For days and days they marched ahead in search of nearest town,
For days and days they had no bread and low became their frown;
They told the boy to show it now, how true he preached to them
That if in prayer he would bow his God would hear him then.

The boy, upheld by strongest Faith, had promised succor soon,
And through the boy spoke God's own breath for great and happy boon.

www.ingramcontent.com/pod-product-compliance
Lightning Source LLC
Chambersburg PA
CBHW031405160426
43196CB00007B/910